DERBYSHIRE IN THE 1930s

A LANTERN SLIDE JOURNEY

DERBYSHIRE IN THE 1930s

A LANTERN SLIDE JOURNEY

The photographs of
ARTHUR ROOKSBY
with text by
DONALD ROOKSBY

TEMPUS

First published 2004

Tempus Publishing Limited
The Mill, Brimscombe Port,
Stroud, Gloucestershire, GL5 2QG
www.tempus-publishing.com

British Library Cataloguing in Publication Data.
A catalogue record for this book is available from the British Library.

ISBN 0 7524 3258 3

Typesetting and origination by Tempus Publishing Limited.
Printed in Great Britain.

(frontispiece)
The packhorse bridge at Holme, on the outskirts of Bakewell, in the mid-1930s. The bridge was built in 1664 but unlike its more familiar counterpart in Bakewell was never widened for modern traffic.

(above)
Arthur Rooksby discusses music to accompany his lantern lectures with his pianist friend J.E. (Eddie) Richards in the 1930s. His slide lectures were always presented with piano accompaniment.

The author and publishers wish to thank Derbyshire County Council for generous support in the production of this book and *Derby Evening Telegraph* for providing help and support during its production.

INTRODUCTION

Derbyshire is a county of beautiful landscapes, and visitors and residents alike have been attracted in their leisure time to its hills and dales for centuries. This collection of photographs features some of the county's best-loved sights and was made in the 1930s by Arthur Rooksby for use in the lantern slide shows he gave at this time. Such slide shows were a popular form of entertainment from late Victorian times to at least the time of the Second World War, enabling local audiences to travel the world without leaving the security of the church or village hall. This is a selective view of the county so there are no industrial, and only a few urban, views in the collection, because this is what audiences would have enjoyed and most expected to see of Derbyshire in a slide show of the time. These delightful photographs provide us with a romantic and picturesque view of Derbyshire at a time, just before the Second World War, when life in the countryside was still conducted at a slower pace than in the towns, and not long before the growth of tourism and the increased use of the motorcar would start to change it all.

Arthur Rooksby was born in Derby in 1892, the son of Samuel Thomas Rooksby and Sarah (née Beall), who had moved from Stamford in Lincolnshire. Arthur's father was a printer by trade but in Derby he developed a small business supplying pens and steel pen nibs to offices in the Derby area. This developed into a wholesale business selling greetings postcards and stationery to local shops, including carded sundries under the trademark, Tip-Top. Arthur trained as a linotype operator and worked at Harpur & Sons, the printers in Friargate, leaving in 1936 to take over his father's business that he operated from his home in Mill Hill Lane. He expanded the business, travelling and delivering orders on foot throughout the town and later, when my wife and I in turn took over and 'motorised' the business in the late 1950s, he retired and 'emigrated' to North Wales.

My father was a keen member of the Derby Photographic Society but ceased to be an active black-and-white photographer in the post-war years. He always treasured his old lantern slides which I eventually inherited. There are over 350 slides, still stored in wooden, Kraft cheese-slice boxes, a large collection of photographic prints and albums of press cuttings about prize-winning prints and items submitted to local and national newspapers and magazines.

Arthur and Sarah were staunch members of Pear Tree Baptist church in Derby and found in the minister, the Revd 'Johnny' Lees, a keen photographic friend. Another member of the chapel was 'Eddie' Richards, a talented musician and pianist who shared in the presentation of the lantern lectures by providing musical accompaniment on the piano. He was also a piano tuner and teacher.

As far as I can remember 'Eddie' Richards never accompanied us on the many trips out to take these photographs. For these we would normally travel by public transport, either by bus or by availing ourselves of one of the vast selection of excursion trains, tantalisingly advertised on handbills hanging in the booking hall of Derby Midland station. Occasionally my parents and I were taken out by the Revd Lees, or by my uncle, Alfred Beard, a deacon at Pear Tree Baptist church, both of whom had cars. My mother was also a photographer and a few of her photographs are included in the book.

Towards the end of the 1930s the Revd C. Sidney Hall came to the church to take over as minister and he, like my parents, was a Christian pacifist. Soon after the outbreak of the 1939–45 war he reported that he had been 'told in a dream' that he should support the country's war effort. This transformation led to my father and mother resigning their membership of the Baptist church to attend meetings of the Society of Friends, the Quakers, eventually becoming Elder and Overseer, respectively, of the Derby Meeting.

I have unfortunately little technical knowledge about the cameras that my parents used at this time. My earliest recollections are of large reflex cameras and a heavy wooden tripod. My father changed later to a Donata folding camera which I believe was a Zeiss Ikon product, as the reflex may well have been too. The earlier photographs were taken on glass plates but later Ilford roll film and film-pack attachments were used. All the prints and lantern slides were processed on a big enlarger and I well remember the kitchen at Mill Hill Lane being transformed into a temporary studio, from time to time, with earthenware dishes of hypo' and other photographic solutions in evidence. In the winter months there were regular engagements to present lantern lectures at various chapels in the Derby area. Eddie Richards wended his way earlier to the venue to tune the piano, knowing that such attention would probably be needed for these often little-used instruments. We would arrive later, my father carrying an attaché case containing the Kraft cheese boxes of slides and a battery-operated cueing device for the lantern operator. This had superseded the 'clicker', an audible cue consisting of a piece of spring steel on a wooden mount, which in turn had taken over from the old command, 'Next slide please'!

Slides of churches and other buildings would be introduced with a few words from my father but the purely landscape pictures, which might include photographs of North Wales and other foreign parts, were projected in sequences with musical accompaniment. Musical pieces such as Chaminade's *Autumn*, Mendelssohn's *Songs Without Words* or Chopin's *Nocturnes* would be played by Eddie on the piano. In the programme there would also be slides of wild flowers or children that were guaranteed to draw 'oohs' and 'ahs' from the audience! Nowadays this type of entertainment seems very quaint to us with our experience of modern film and television but there is a lot to be said for simple pleasures. Even modern photo-slide shows can seem very cold by comparison, with their slick audio-visual techniques and recorded music, but times change.

This book is a picture of Derbyshire in the 1930s, but also it is a tribute to my father and others like him who sought to share their love of the countryside with others through photographs. I dedicate this book to the memory of Arthur and Emma Rooksby who, with Eddie Richards, taught me to appreciate photography, the countryside and music. and to my wife, Margaret, who gave me great support while preparing this book, but sadly passed away before its publication. All royalties will be donated to the *Derby Evening Telegraphs'* Magic Million Fund for cancer treatment equipment.

Donald A. Rooksby
Eglwysbach, Conwy
March 2004

A young Donald Rooksby examines his father's reflex plate camera, used to take many of the earlier photographs in the collection, in around 1929.

All Saints' church, Dale Abbey. This tiny and unusual church, some 25ft square, sits under the same roof as a farmhouse and the one time Bluebell Inn which closed in 1820. The interior is a jumble of seventeenth-century box pews with a pulpit of 1634. The arrangement of pulpit, lectern and clerk's pew behind the altar is the only such instance to be found in a church still in use. There is a gallery, accessed from outside. Nearby is the chancel arch of St Mary's Abbey, the sole surviving fragment of the Premonstratensian monastery founded here in around 1200.

(left)
The parish church of St Michael and St Mary, Melbourne, is described by Pevsner as 'one of the most ambitious Norman parish churches in England, and its interior is as impressive and as well preserved as any', though he goes on to consider the exterior as 'unfortunate'. He refers in particular to the tithe barn which stands very near to the west front and the incomplete west towers to which pyramidal roofs were added in 1862. These 'pepper pots' were removed in 1955.

(right)
A misericord detail in All Saints' church, Bakewell. My father enjoyed photographing unusual church furnishings and ornaments and I too acquired his fascination for misericords – the hinged seats of choir stalls that enabled choristers to support themselves during long periods of standing in church. Bakewell has a fine selection of misericords, old and new, and this witty example is based on the political slogan of Wilkie Collins – 'Three Acres [achers] and a Cow!'

(above)
'The Lonely Beauty', one of only two surviving old carved bench-ends in St Michael's, Crich.

(left)
All Saints' parish church, Sawley.

These evocative photographs of old-fashioned farmyard scenes were taken (opposite) at a farm off Morley Road, Chaddesden, and (right) at Wingfield Manor.

(top)

This marble boar was a great favourite in the Derby Arboretum for over 100 years until it was damaged by shrapnel when a bomb destroyed the nearby bandstand during an air-raid. It was never replaced but there must be many an old photograph in family albums around Derby of children posing like this with the statue.

(left)

This view in Markeaton Park was photographed in the 1930s following a period of great activity during a flood-relief programme by Derby Corporation. Alongside this track was a group of narrow gauge 0-4-0 tank locomotives awaiting removal after use during the construction work.

(opposite)

A misty morning in Derby Arboretum. The landscaped park was given to the people of Derby by Joseph Strutt in 1840 and was possibly the first public park in the country.

(left)

St Mary's Gate House was built in the 1720s for William Osborne, and was sold by Walter Evans of Darley Abbey to the Baptists for conversion into a chapel. It was subsequently sold in 1937 to the Kennings group and demolished the following year. The magnificent gates, made by Derby craftsman Robert Bakewell, were fortunately saved and are preserved at the west entrance to the Cathedral.

(right)

The parish church of All Saints' was elevated to cathedral status in 1927, just fifty years before Derby became a city on 28 July 1977. All Saints' magnificent 178ft tower was built in the early sixteenth century – the next highest parish church tower in the country to Boston, Lincolnshire. The remaining part of the church was demolished in 1723 and rebuilt by James Gibbs, designer of St Martin-in-the-Fields, London. As a child I made several ascents of the tower on open days and recall the time when one of the pinnacles was toppled by a stray barrage balloon cable during the war. This photograph is from the early 1930s before trams gave way to trolleybuses. The timber-framed building is the sixteenth-century Dolphin Inn and nearer to the Cathedral on the left was Proctor's herbalist shop, a fascinating old emporium of mysterious jars, natural remedies and vegetarian products. I remember they were stockists for Mapletons' fruitarian cakes.

The Nottingham Castle Inn in St Michael's Lane, Derby, in the early 1930s. Derby, like many cities, suffered the demolition of many of its important old buildings during the twentieth century, when replacement took precedence over restoration in a drive for improvement and modernisation. This building was demolished as recently as 1962.

(left)
St Mary's Chapel-on-the-Bridge is one of only six surviving bridge chapels in England. 'St Mary's on the Brigge' was built in the fifteenth century and was restored in the early 1930s following the efforts of the Derbyshire Archaeological Society.

(top)
Derby County Gaol (renamed HM Derby Prison in the 1880s) was demolished in 1929. The prison was designed by Francis Goodwin, the architect of St John's church in Bridge Street and was built in 1828. Its Doric façade survives today, facing Vernon Street, and now forms the entrance to a commercial estate. My father would have photographed the prison's demolition with special interest because he was held in custody there for a while as a conscientious objector during the First World War.

(above)
Mill Hill Lane, Derby, was synonymous for many with the dreaded schools clinic, which included a dentist's surgery at Temple House. Mill Hill Lane was also where my family home was situated. The summit of the lane, which branches south-west from Normanton Road and is roughly parallel with the Burton Road, was greatly changed in about 1930 when the lodge and gates were demolished to provide an entrance to the new clinic. There is now a new entrance drive here to the new St Joseph's church and school on the slope above Burton Road.

(left)
The Mayor's Parlour in Tenant Street. There is no evidence that there was ever any mayoral use but Derby's longest-serving Recorder (1661-1703) lived here at one time. The Derby historian, Maxwell Craven, believes it to have been built in 1483 with a 'massive oak newel staircase and a wealth of linen-fold panelling'. In this photograph the building clearly shows signs of neglect and deterioration and was around the time in the 1930s that The Derby Archaeological Society had offered to purchase the building, bringing about a temporary stay of execution. It was finally demolished in 1948 for a development scheme that never came into being.

(left)
In 1902 the foundation stone was laid for a new Baptist chapel on Pear Tree Road, on the corner of Goodale Street and opposite St Thomas's church, to replace an earlier one in Rutland Street. The chapel opened in July 1903 and this photograph was taken around 1930 when the Revd J. H. Lees commenced his ministry.

(right)
Pear Tree Baptist Sunday school anniversary celebration in 1921. This was an annual event when wooden decking would be erected over the baptistry to accommodate the scholars. Whitsuntide Treats were another regular item on the Sunday school calendar: children would travel by horse-drawn dray from the Rutland Street schoolrooms to Normanton Recreation Ground. On these occasions we congregated in the schoolrooms for a celebratory tea and I recall some scholars would stick cream buns on the underside of the trestle tables!

(left)
Derby has a number of public parks and none, to my mind, is more attractive than Darley Park. Like Markeaton, it was designed by William Emes. The hall and park, which became a public park in the 1930s, was the family home of the Evans family who developed the riverside mills in the eighteenth and nineteenth centuries. During the war the hall was the temporary home of Derby Central School for boys – a more idyllic site than Abbey Street! Pupils were not allowed into the maze behind the trees in the photograph, nor to visit the banana tree in the greenhouses, both of which we had enjoyed on family visits before the war. Sadly, the hall went into decline after the school moved to Breadsall Hill Top in 1958 and it was demolished in 1962.

(right)
This contented group of porkers were photographed at a farm off the Morley Road in Chaddesden.

(above)
Swarkeston Hall, alongside the river Trent, is an elegant three-gabled manor house with mullioned windows, built in the mid-seventeenth century.

(opposite)
The Summer House at Swarkestone in about 1935. This unusual building is also known as The Grandstand, the Pavilion and the Balcony and it overlooks the Cuttle, a rectangular enclosure which may have been used for sporting activities or even bull-baiting. The building has now been acquired by the Landmark Trust and converted for holiday accommodation. The gateway is a survivor from the long-demolished manor house.

The tithe barn at Swarkestone has been converted into living accommodation since this photograph was taken in the 1930s. The manor house stood close by.

The old mill at Melbourne. Beyond Church Walk and past the grounds of Melbourne Hall is this old mill. The hall and gardens have become a popular tourist attraction in recent decades.

St James. An interesting feature of Swarkestone church is the Harpur Chapel where there are two tomb-chests with effigies of members of the Harpur family, Richard (d. 1577) and Sir John (d. 1627), with their wives. When this photograph was taken in the mid-1930s there was an interesting relic on the south window ledge of the chapel – an ancient helmet surmounted by a rather worm-eaten, carved wooden boar. The helmet was stolen during a burglary some years ago but later the boar emblem was recovered and is now in safe-keeping at nearby Calke Abbey (National Trust), which was built in 1703 as the new seat of the Harpur family.

St Michael's church, Stanton-by-Bridge. A famous medieval causeway connects Swarkestone and Stanton across a frequently flooded piece of land. It is almost a mile in length and a local benefactor, Sir John Port, who founded Repton School and Etwall Hospital, left money for its maintenance. Before the construction of the Cavendish Bridge at Shardlow in about 1758 this was the main route from London to the north-west.

(above)
The church and cross at Repton.

(opposite)
The tithe barn at Melbourne was built in the thirteenth century.

(left)
These old thatched cottages survive today in Potter Street, Melbourne.

(right)
This stretch of the river Trent, east of Willington, is now overshadowed by Willington power station but, seventy years ago, it was a very pastoral scene with cattle cooling off in the water.

This photograph of the old tithe barn in Melbourne shows how close it stands to the west end of the church. The original thirteenth-century building has been added to in more recent years, particularly in the eighteenth century. The 'pepper pot' towers that once adorned the west end of the church are clearly seen.

This old cruck-framed cottage still exists on the High Street in Melbourne.

A fine row of cottages in Melbourne, each from a different period.

Church Walk, Melbourne. Leaving the village this walk leads towards Melbourne Pool and, beyond, towards the cool shade of Intake Wood.

This photograph shows to full effect the sturdiness of the Norman piers and ornamented arches that form the nave of Melbourne church. There is a clerestory passage above.

(opposite)
Melbourne station in the late 1920s. An ex-Midland Railway Johnson 2-4-0 waits to haul its train back to Derby, tender-first, on the Ashby branch line. The passenger service ceased in the early 1930s but continued for freight and enjoyed a stay of execution as the Melbourne Military Railway during the Second World War.

(left)
The west door of Melbourne church.

(right)
A view of Melbourne village from the far side of the pool with the church in the centre and the hall on the right. Trips to Melbourne were a favourite family excursion by Trent bus in the 1930s, which cost us two adult returns at 1s 1d each and a child return at 7d. I remember clearly the conductor would issue two sixpenny tickets and three sevenpenny ones, standing in a slightly bow-legged stance as bus conductors were wont to do to steady themselves!

Ingleby is on the south side of the river Trent, a mile south of Barrow-on-Trent. The Anchor church is near the bank of the river, possibly a natural cave which has been enlarged into two rooms with windows. Tradition has it that it was occupied by an Anchorite monk, Bernard, in the twelfth century.

(opposite)
Fishing in the pool at Melbourne has always been a favourite pastime for children.

Three young fishermen examine their catch of minnows at Melbourne pool.

(left)
St Wilfred's church, Barrow-on-Trent.

(right)
The Ticknall lock-up or roundhouse. A local public house landlady, it is said, found that one of her keys fitted the lock which could be used to release her customers! Ticknall was once connected to Ashby by a horse-drawn tramway which crossed the road in the village by a narrow stone bridge.

Three miles north-east of Weston-on-Trent, the Trent and Mersey Canal meets the river at Shardlow, once an important inland port. Now it is a popular boating centre and a marina was opened in 1975. The old Clock Warehouse shown here at the junction of the waterways was built in 1780 and is now rebuilt as Hoskin's Wharf, a public house and restaurant.

(top)
The Cat and Fiddle windmill at Dale Abbey is the only working postmill, turning to face the wind on a central post, in Derbyshire. It has been restored by Stanton Ironworks which owns and maintains it.

(right)
St Andrew's church, Twyford. An old chain-operated ferry across the Trent from Repton to Twyford remained in use until it was destroyed by floods in 1963. Twyford church is unprepossessing from the outside. The nave was encased in brick in the eighteenth century and became overgrown with ivy and Pevsner's account of the building concludes, 'May no purist insist on its removal'. The most striking feature inside is this simple Norman chancel arch.

Etwall post office in Main Street is probably of eighteenth-century origin, with later neo-Jacobean gables. The business was one of my customers in my wholesale stationery days. This view dates from 1930 when it was safe to take a photograph from the roadway, even though the main road to the Potteries passed through the village.

The Sir John Port Hospital in Etwall was founded in the mid-sixteenth century and rebuilt in 1681. Twelve dwellings, four on each of three blocks facing a central courtyard, were built to accommodate old men of the village. The almshouses lie directly behind the churchyard of St Helen's church.

All Saints' church in Dalbury, a small village a mile or so north of Etwall.

Osiers alongside a stream near Dalbury in the mid-1930s.

(opposite)
Marchington is a small village just over the county border into Staffordshire and this is a group of its young inhabitants in the late 1920s.

(above)
A quaint old shop with shuttered windows in Ludgate Street, Tutbury, in the early 1930s. The village was, and still is, a popular visiting place for Derby families, not least because it has a castle.

The scattered village of Radbourne is situated between Mackworth and Etwall. Radburne (*sic*) Hall lies south of the village and St Andrew's church stands in the grounds. 'The Old Hare and Hounds', a one-time inn, is situated on a lane to the north and has been delightfully restored by its present owners.

(top)
The feature of the 'hidden' village of Osmaston, a short distance west of the Derby to Ashbourne road and actually on the old road to Ashbourne, is its thatched cottages. Even some quite recent houses and the village hall, erected in 1937 by Sir Ian Walker-Oakover, are thatched. Osmaston manor was demolished in 1966.

(right)
A pretty woodland lane and ford close to the village of Osmaston.

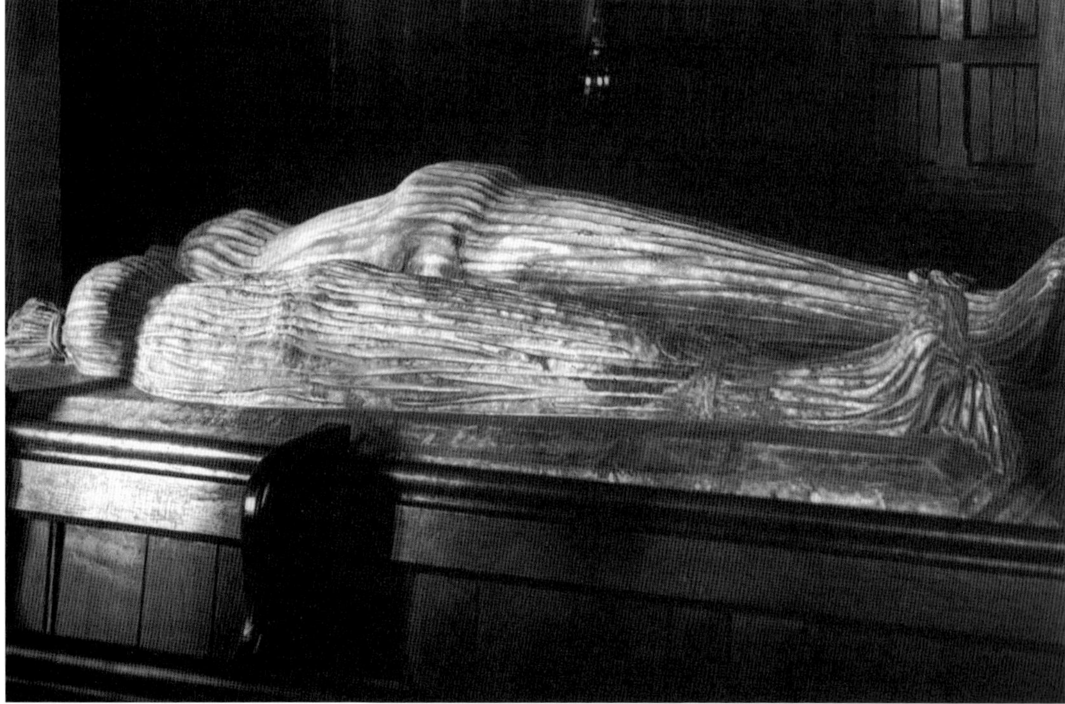

(top)
Fenny Bentley manor house photographed in 1933. The original part of the hall is the square medieval tower, all that now remains of the Beresford family's fortified, moated house. The remaining 'new' building is a seventeenth-century construction.

(left)
In St Edmund's church, Fenny Bentley, is this unusual memorial. It was carved in 1473 and bears the effigies of Thomas and Agnes Beresford of Fenny Bentley wrapped in shrouds. A possible explanation for this unusual depiction is that the deceased were not known to the stone mason commissioned to produce the memorial, nor were their likenesses available to him, so portraying them covered was the only solution. Images of their twenty-one children appear on the sides of the tomb.

Ashbourne Grammar School, founded in 1585, was once the home of the Queen Elizabeth Grammar School. Although these school buildings still grace the main road into town, the school was transferred some years ago to a new building north-east of the town.

The beautiful unspoilt village of Tissington is approached from the Ashbourne road along this attractive half-mile avenue of trees.

Tissington Hall has been the home of the FitzHerbert family for almost 400 years. The house was built in 1609 and the wrought-iron entrance gates were made by Robert Bakewell of Derby in about 1720. The hall has been open to the public since 1998.

Well dressing in Derbyshire is a very old tradition and is seen in many of the county's villages but Tissington is considered to be the pioneer of the custom. It is known that wells were decorated here in 1350 but the custom probably dates back much earlier as a thanksgiving for the blessing of water. Every Ascension Day six wells in the village are decorated. The practice continues today and each year thousands of visitors come to see them. This is Hands well photographed in 1933.

(left)
Town well, 1934.

(centre)
Hall well, 1934.

(right)
Coffin well, 1933.

(top)
The famous stepping stones at Dovedale. An ideal route to see and appreciate the Dove valley is to walk from Hartington via Beresford Dale, Wolfscote Dale, Milldale and Dovedale. A short extension from the Stepping Stones below Thorpe Cloud (942ft) to Thorpe village completes the traverse. I recall my father always bemoaning the fact that visitors who had seen the Stepping Stones, and maybe crossed the Dove the easy way by donkey, had not been to Dovedale! After leaving this point by the Stepping Stones the Twelve Apostles rocks are passed on the left, followed shortly by the natural archway of Reynard's Cave on the right side. Then Lion's Head Rock is followed, on the Staffordshire side, by Ilam Rock opposite Pickering Tor. Beyond is Hall Dale, shortly before the shallow caves of Dove Holes and ahead, across the Viator's Bridge, is the hamlet of Milldale.

(left)
A group of donkeys await customers for a trip across the river. Nowadays visitors have to walk across.

The riverside footpath at Dovedale.

(top)
The Viator's (wayfarer's) Bridge at Milldale was a favourite spot of Isaak Walton (author of *The Compleat Angler*) and Charles Cotton, whose 'fishing temple' was built in 1674 and still exists in Beresford Dale.

(left)
Dovedale, a place for contemplation. From a very early age I was a regular visitor to Dovedale, which thankfully has changed little over the years, except perhaps for the number of visitors. The riverside footpath has been improved and lost some of its charm in the process but, in the 1930s, it could be very wet and muddy after rainy periods.

One of the most popular viewpoints in Dovedale is the Lion's Head Rock. The rock bears a remarkable likeness to a lion when viewed from upstream.

A beautifully carved rood screen in St Edmund's church, Fenny Bentley, which is believed to date from the early sixteenth century.

Temperance Gell's Folly at Hopton, near Carsington. This quaint little house was associated with nearby Hopton Hall, home of the Gell family.

(left)
St Mary's church, Wirksworth.

(right)
Wirksworth's parish church is unusual in having two fonts. One (bottom) in the north transept, described by Pevsner as 'a large, plain, impressive cauldron', stands on four legs and is of Norman origin. The other (top) is ornate in design and carries the date 1662.

The Barley Mow is still the village inn at Kirk Ireton.

(left)
A corbel of a sheep with a human face carved on a wall in Holy Trinity church, Kirk Ireton.

(right)
Holy Trinity church at Kirk Ireton has traces of Norman architecture.

In the mid-1930s my parents became acquainted with a Mr Talbot who had a smallholding one mile up a lane from Wirksworth's main street, just south of the road to Carsington and Ashbourne. Many happy hours were spent at this rural retreat.

(top)

A popular walk from the north end of Duffield, near the site of the twelfth-century Duffield Castle with its keep of similar proportions to the White Tower in London and Colchester's Norman keep, leads past the golf course to the hill known as the Chevin. This elevated viewpoint overlooks Duffield, Milford, Belper and the Ecclesbourne valley to the west.

(left)

As you approach Duffield on the A6 travelling north, a minor road branches off by the Baptist chapel towards Little Eaton and crosses first the Derby-Sheffield railway line and then the river Derwent by this elegant bridge beside the Bridge Inn.

The Cromford Canal at Whatstandwell. The 5½ miles of the Cromford Canal between Cromford and Ambergate were restored by the Cromford Canal Society but ownership was transferred to Derbyshire County Council in 1974. To walk along the towpath of the canal today is to step back into the 1930s when this photograph was taken.

The river bridge at Whatstandwell. It is generally agreed that the strange name of this village is derived from Walter (Wat) Stonewell, a tenant of Darley Abbey in the late fourteenth century. The Derwent valley around Whatstandwell is interesting in that it is threaded by four modes of transport. The river came first, then the road, followed by the Cromford Canal in the late eighteenth century. Finally, the railway arrived in the nineteenth century. In this picture the A6 road sweeps over the Derwent just below the village, where the roads from Alderwasley and Wirksworth join from the west and the hill to Crich and Ripley ascends in the distance.

Chadwick Nick, near Crich. From the road between Whatstandwell and Crich a lane branches off towards Fritchley. It passes through Chadwick Nick, known locally as Chaddickernick, and passes over the track bed of the narrow-gauge tramway between Crich quarries and Ambergate limeworks. The system closed in 1957 and the track was taken for use on the Tal-y-llyn Railway in North Wales. Some loaded wagons can be seen in the middle distance.

A distant view of Crich Stand. Situated just north of Crich village is a memorial to '11,409 men of all rank of the Sherwood Foresters' who were lost in the First World War. The monument, the third to stand here and completed in 1923, stands 950ft above sea level on the cliffs of the erstwhile Crich quarries. The National Tramway Museum is now located on this cliff top too, where the façade of the old Derby Assembly Rooms has been re-erected. The flashing beacon of the Stand is visible at night from the A6 and for miles around.

ROBIN HOOD COTTAGE
IN THE HAMLET OF ROBIN HOOD
IS SEEN 'ABOVE' THE AUSTIN CAR.
MY MOTHER LIVED THERE
IN 1912 WHEN SHE WAS 11 years old

Scarthin, Cromford village. Reached via a narrow lane from the Square with its post office and famous bookshop, Scarthin overlooks the Greyhound pond at Cromford, which is viewed here from Water Lane, a scene that has changed little for generations. Water Lane continues to the Via Gellia road connecting Cromford with Grange Mill and the Ashbourne-Buxton road. The Via Gellia retains much of its charm but is sadly marred by the amount of heavy traffic which passes through today.

A short distance from the wharf in Cromford at the northern end of the Cromford Canal is this bridge over the river Derwent – curious in that the arches on one side are pointed and on the other side rounded. Adjoining the bridge are a small fishing temple and the remains of a fifteenth-century bridge chapel. St Mary's church, built for Richard Arkwright in 1797, is nearby and, nearer the village, is Arkwright's historic water-powered cotton mill of 1771.

The river Derwent at Matlock Bath where tourists have been drawn to the sights and the entertainments for more than a hundred years.

The river at Matlock Bath.

Matlock Bath has for many years offered the kind of entertainments, cafés and illuminated walks that are usually only seen at seaside resorts. In the 1930s among the visitor attractions were this unique fountain and the so-called Petrifying Well. At the 'Well' domestic and personal artefacts could be left to become encrusted with limestone deposits and 'petrified'.

(top)
Cromford Bridge with Willersley Castle in the background. The 'castle' was built by Richard Arkwright as the family home but he died before it was finished. It is now a Methodist guesthouse and conference centre.

(left)
The Gregory Tunnel on the Cromford Canal is half-way between Whatstandwell and Leawood pumping station. Although there is a towpath through this short tunnel it was apparently the custom to manhandle the barges through and walk the horses over the footpath above the tunnel.

Reflections in the river at Matlock Bath.

EACOCK

(opposite)
The Peacock Hotel at Rowsley. This famous hostelry has changed little in outside appearance since this photograph was taken in around 1929, except that the trees have been tidied up. The Peacock was built by John Stephenson as a private residence in 1652 and it became a hotel in 1828.

(right)
St John's Chapel is tucked away on Cliff Road, Matlock Dale. It was built in 1897 as a chapel of ease for St Giles, Matlock and built to the design of Sir Guy Dauber.

(left)
The bridge over the River Wye at Bakewell. A pleasant riverside walk passes the river bridge towards the showfield where the celebrated annual Bakewell Show is held on the first Thursday in August – one of the best one-day country shows in the country.

(right)
An unusual, fourteenth-century misericord in Bakewell church.

(opposite)
The south porch of Bakewell church in 1933. Bakewell curch is one of no fewer than thirty-two Derbyshire churches dedicated to All Saints'. St Michael and St Mary come next with twenty-two and nineteen, respectively. Much of this church dates from the thirteenth century although it was extensively restored in the nineteenth century. There was an earlier Saxon church on the site.

Stone coffins photographed alongside the south porch at Bakewell church.

Bakewell and the river Wye. Bakewell was always a popular venue for family excursions – Ashford-in-the-Water, Monsal Dale and Lathkill Dale were within walking distance and of course the church was a great attraction to my father. At the end of the day we would trudge the half-mile up the hill to the railway station for the return train to Derby.

Bakewell and its bridge, built in the thirteenth century as a packhorse bridge and widened in the nineteenth to take the increasing traffic. A short distance into the town today one passes one of several Bakewell Pudding shops, the home of what we always referred to as a Bakewell Tart. My mother made a worthy imitation that was eaten with relish and seemed to be preferred to the secret recipe of the original!

Sheepwash Bridge at Ashford-in-the-Water near Bakewell. It takes its name from an adjacent area of river used for washing sheep in years gone by. There remains a sheep pound nearby.

(top)
Ashford-in-the-Water is a popular summertime venue for strolling visitors today but it was a much quieter village in the 1930s.

(left)
The river Wye near Ashford-in-the-Water.

(opposite)
The River Wye meandering down through Chee Dale, Millers Dale, Cressbrook Dale and Monsal Dale in 1933. At Monsal Head express trains once burst out of the tunnel and crossed the river on a spectacular viaduct on their way from Derby to Manchester, but now the trains have gone and the track bed is a walking route, the Monsal Trail.

The Plague Cottages at Eyam look today very much as they did in the 1930s, so complete has been the preservation of this row of houses. In 1665 the plague was brought from London in a contaminated box of clothes to one of these cottages. The epidemic was contained within the village through the diligent efforts of the rector William Mompesson, who imposed a regime of isolation from the outside world. No fewer than 257 inhabitants of Eyam succumbed and the event is still remembered every August at a service in Cucklet Dell where outdoor services were held during the plague. The tower of St Lawrence's church can be seen beyond the cottages.

Eyam parish church. The sundial on the porch is reputed to date from 1775 and it shows not only local time but also the time in different parts of the world. Another important relic in Eyam churchyard is the virtually complete Saxon cross.

Wingfield Manor is the county's great romantic ruin. It was built in the middle of the fifteenth century as home for Ralph, Lord Cromwell, and sits on a hill near the village of South Wingfield. This is the south wall of the great solar or parlour.

The barn seen here at Wingfield Manor may not have been used as a barn as it has a fireplace, suggesting other uses. English Heritage is now responsible for upkeep of the manor and suggests that the ground floor could have been a store and the upper floor a courtroom, like Preston Patrick Hall in Cumbria. The Austin van parked in the courtyard here in 1933 looks brand new.

(opposite)
Then, as now, Wingfield Manor housed a working farm and there are still farm buildings scattered amongst the ruins between the inner and the outer courtyards. This picture was taken outside the farm buildings adjacent to the farmhouse in around 1929.

(above)
Wingfield Manor viewed from the High Tower. A considerable amount of clearing of the site has taken place since these photographs were taken in the 1930s. The larger of two ground-floor rooms housed a six-seater latrine as evidenced by the timber sockets in the walls. The English Heritage guide suggests that a cistern could have flushed the latrine making it the earliest known water closet.

The archway of the gatehouse of Wingfield Manor connects the outer and inner courtyards. The coat of arms of Lord Cromwell, the original owner, can be seen above the gateway.

The beautiful wooded paths of Lathkill Dale, a mile or two south of Bakewell. A rough track from Monyash, once a thriving lead-mining centre, descends to Low Wood and follows the river below Over Haddon and past the delightfully named Conksbury Bridge to Alport, near Youlgreave.

Cello with warming-pan obbligato! In the 1920s and 30s the Adult School Union organised weekends at The Briars guesthouse, situated between Crich and Fritchley. This was a Quaker vegetarian establishment owned by Arthur and Katie Ludlow and these weekends were happy social occasions, laced with humour, as this picture shows. In this photograph taken by my mother, Mr Poole plays the cello to my father's warming-pan accompaniment. A Sunny Jim doll, the trade mark of the breakfast cereal, Force, is tucked into the cello.